THE ISRAELI/PALESTINIAN CONFLICT

Sharon Thompson

THE ISRAELI/PALESTINIAN CONFLICT

© 2024 Sharon Thompson

Published by Texianer Verlag
Johannesstraße 12
78609 Tuningen
Germany
www.texianer.com

ISBN: 978-3-910667-17-4

ABOUT THE AUTHOR

Sharon Thompson and her husband of sixty years, Gordon, a retired dairy farmer, are the parents of six daughters (and now six sons-in-law) who have blessed them with twenty grandchildren and nine great-grandchildren. Her family is her greatest love and joy. Her hope is that this study guide will play a role in advancing a worldwide discussion that will lead to a reclaimed world of love, peace, and justice for all people everywhere.

THE ISRAELI/PALESTINIAN CONFLICT

By Sharon Thompson

NARRATOR: The Israeli/Palestinian conflict did not begin on October 7, 2023. It has been ongoing for over a hundred years. It started with the birth of Zionism. Zionism was born in response to an especially severe attack on Russian Jews in 1881. The Zionist solution envisioned the creation of an independent Jewish state in Palestine that would require the expulsion of the indigenous population. The Zionists were secular European Jews and knew that their goal could only be realized through violence. The Zionist state they envisioned was patterned after the European powers of their day. The Zionist movement has always been backed by a major world power (and the Western world, in general)—first by Great Britain and then by the United States which were both seeking their own strategic goals without any real concern for the Jewish people.

The basis of the conflict between the Israelis and the Palestinians is that they both feel they are the rightful owners of the same piece of land. To emphasize this point, two speakers, one representing the Zionist/Israeli point of view and the other representing the Palestinian point of view, will speak. We will first hear from the Zionist/Israeli point of view of why the land is rightfully theirs.

ZIONIST/ISRAELI: The Jewish people have a relationship of more than 37 centuries duration with their historic homeland. Whether living there or unjustly evicted from it and trying to return, the Jewish claim has never been surrendered and never will be. While Arabs control a vast territory and many nations, there is no Jewish state other than tiny Israel. Nowhere else is Hebrew spoken. No other nation is dedicated to the survival of the Jewish people. And the experience of many centuries has shown that the Jews cannot survive without a national home of their own. The Jews have nowhere else to go.

PALESTINIAN: The Palestinians are descendents of the Canaanites who predated the Jews in the region and descendents of the Arabs who came after. Therefore, the Palestinians have the earliest and the longest claim to the land. The ancient Hebrews took possession of the land by conquest, which was no more moral than the subsequent conquests that evicted them. The final eviction of the Jews was perpetrated by the Romans. Their suffering over the centuries was at the hands of European Christians and others. If the Jews deserve compensation for their suffering, let them seek it from the perpetrators, not from the Palestinian Arabs who were innocent bystanders until Zionism forced them to defend their home. Since the Jews were evicted from Jerusalem in 135 A. D., almost every bit of real estate on the planet has changed hands. If all nations were to adopt this strange Zionist logic, the world would be in utter chaos.

NARRATOR: The land of Israel, formerly Palestine, formerly Canaan, has had a long and eventful history. In ancient times, it served as a land bridge between Mesopotamia in the East and Egypt in the West. Through it ran the important trade routes of the ancient world — east to west and south to the Persian Gulf. Its strategic location gave it an importance far greater than its small size and nominal natural resources might suggest it would have. Because of this, it lay like a pawn between Egypt and the great powers of Mesopotamia.

Canaan, later to be Palestine, had permanent settlements by about 7,000 B.C.E. But because of its location, from this time up until the mid-twentieth century, almost 9,000 years, Palestine was controlled by one or another of the great powers of the day. There were two brief exceptions, one of them notable.

At the time of the Iron Age, about 1,000 B.C.E. Egypt and the Hittites to the east had fought a long, exhaustive war. At its conclusion, neither had the means or the energy to control Palestine. Into this political vacuum flowed the landless peoples of the desert fringes and others. They fought amongst themselves for pieces of land and the mini-nations of Philistia, Phoenicia, Syria, Israel, Judah, Moab, Ammon, and Edom were established at this time. I am noting this event because one of these tiny nations, the United Kingdom of Israel and Judah later gave rise to the Jewish people of which we will be concerned. This brief interlude in Palestine—the Small Nation Era—lasted about 300 years. Israel controlled the region for about 60 of those years.

The twentieth century and World War I brought major changes to Palestine, but first we have to look at the beginnings of the Zionist movement which was to have a profound effect on the history of Palestine. In 1881 an outbreak of attacks against the Jews in Russia was especially severe. One of the responses to these attacks was the birth of Zionism. The Zionists saw the only solution to anti-semitism as being the creation of an independent Jewish state. The obvious location for this state (at least to the Zionists) was the land of Palestine, the site of the only other previous Jewish state. Between 1882 and 1903, 25,000 Jews migrated to Palestine.

Independently, a Hungarian Jew, Theodor Herzl, came to the same conclusion as the Russian Jews, but with one major exception: he felt a program of gradual Jewish in-migration was doomed as the native population would surely oppose it. He felt it was necessary to seek an "assured supremacy" in advance. He proposed that one of the major powers declare a territory in advance as available for Jewish state building. The Ottoman Turks who controlled Palestine at the time were unreceptive, so Herzl and the Zionists turned to the British. On November 2, 1917, the British Cabinet adopted a statement favoring the establishment of a Jewish national home in Palestine. It was called the Balfour Declaration. To give you a better idea of how the Israelis and the Palestinians view the Balfour Declaration, the Palestinian speaker will speak first, followed by the Zionist/Israeli speaker.

PALESTINIAN: The Balfour Declaration is no less than theft,

deception, and racism in the service of imperialism. The theft is the theft of Palestine from its rightful Arab owners. The deception is a series of false promises made by Westerners to Arabs. During World War I, Britain promised to help the Arabs get their independence if the Arabs helped Britain win the war. The Arabs kept their end of the bargain, but the British never delivered independence. Instead, Britain and France secretly divided the Arab world between themselves while Britain further conspired to award Palestine to the Zionists.

The racism exudes even from the Balfour Declaration itself. The text doesn't mention the Arabs, but refers to "the existing non-Jewish communities in Palestine," as if there was a small non-Jewish minority there when the population was 90% Arab. This reflects the prevailing anti-Arab racism of the British.

The imperialism part of the equation is the attitude of Westerners that the non-European portions of the planet exist for the use and convenience of Europeans. What could be more imperialistic than a declaration that says, in essence: we're going to conquer this territory over here, and we'll assign it as a homeland to these people and we won't even ask the people who live there what they think about it.

Balfour's statement not only reeks of arrogance, racism, and Western imperialism, but the declaration cannot be taken seriously because Britain lacks the legal and moral right to dispose of Palestine. We Arabs claim the right of a population to decide the fate of the country which we have occupied throughout history. It is obvious this right of immemorial possession is inalienable. It cannot be overruled either by the circumstances that Palestine has been governed by the Ottomans for 400 years, or that Britain had conquered the land during World War I, or that a Jewish state has been established in a part of it by brute force.

ZIONIST/ISRAELI: Things looked bleak early in the twentieth century for the imperiled Jewish people. But, as always, God was on our side and knew our needs better than we did. Palestine was part of the Ottoman Empire and the sultan had rejected the Zionist project. World War I, with all its horrors, was actually an answer to Zionist prayers. Control over Palestine passed from Ottoman to British jurisdiction. Just as this was about to happen, the British government changed hands. The new government featured a prime minister, David Lloyd George, and a foreign secretary, Alfred James Balfour, both of whom had previously concluded that the Jews must have a home at the site of the ancient Jewish state. Who can doubt that God was looking out for his people? The timely issuing of the Balfour Declaration and subsequent world events attest to this.

NARRATOR: Actually, in issuing the Balfour Declaration, the British were not primarily concerned with the plight of the Jews. Rather, they saw it as a means to help themselves win World War I. Britain was concerned to keep Russia in the war on the Allied side and to encourage the United States to enter the war. They hoped Jewish influence in these countries would tip the scales of public opinion in that direction. It did not help in the case of Russia, but it did help to gain support for the British and their Zionist cause in the United States.

But the Balfour Declaration was just one of several promises the British had made to help ensure their victory in World War I. The Palestinians had also been promised their independence in return for helping the British war effort. During the period between World War I (1914-1919) and 1948, Palestine was what was termed a class A mandate. They were a country whose independence was provisionally recognized, but subject to advice and assistance from Britain (who held the mandate) until they were able to stand alone. They were in a transition stage — being groomed, so to speak, for independence and eventual self-rule.

So the British had promised a national home in Palestine to the Jews and had promised independence to the Palestinians. How could this possibly work out? It couldn't. Following World

War I, which ended in 1919, the League of Nations was established to maintain world peace. The League of Nations awarded the Palestine Mandate to Britain in 1922 which would remain in effect until 1948. Britain (at this point), as well as the League of Nations, was pro-Zionist, and heavily favored the Zionist project at the expense of the indigenous Palestinians. Let's hear the response to this situation, first from the Zionist/Israeli side and then from the Palestinian side.

ZIONIST/ISRAELI: We were fortunate to have the backing of the British government, the world's leading power at the time, that had issued the Balfour Declaration. We couldn't have been more pleased when the Palestine Mandate included the Balfour Declaration, word for word, thus, we were given an international pledge to uphold the provisions of the Balfour Declaration. In the Preamble of the Mandate, the Jewish people, and only the Jewish people, are described as having a historic connection to Palestine. The Mandate also laid out the key means for establishing and expanding our national home that we were reconstituting. We also had the financial support of the Jewish Colonization Association (CJA) whose wealthy patrons helped to relocate beleaguered European Jews.

PALESTINIAN: As soon as we were able to do so in the wake of World War I, we began to organize politically in opposition both to British rule and to the obvious favoritism of the Zionist movement that was inherent in the Palestine Mandate. Petitions were brought before the British government, to the Paris Peace Conference, and to the League of Nations, all to no avail. We convened a series of seven Palestine Arab congresses planned by a country-wide network of Muslim and Christian societies which were held from 1919 until 1928. These congresses put forward a consistent series of demands focused on independence for Arab Palestine, rejection of the Balfour Declaration, support for majority rule, and ending unlimited Jewish immigration and land purchases. When all of these official actions failed, and the common people rose up in protest, they were beaten back by the power of the British army.

NARRATOR: The experience in Palestine was dissimilar to that of most other colonized peoples in this area in that the Palestine Mandate brought an influx of foreign settlers whose mission it was to take over the country. However, between 1926 and 1932, the Jewish population ceased to grow, leveling off at about 18% of the total population. At that point, the Zionist project looked as if it might never attain the critical demographic mass that could fulfill the Zionist mission of Palestine becoming a Jewish state.

Everything changed in 1933 with the rise to power in Germany of the Nazis, who immediately began to persecute and drive out the well-established Jewish community. In 1935 alone, more than 60,000 Jewish immigrants came to Palestine. With discriminatory immigration laws in place in the United States, the United Kingdom, and other countries, many German Jews had nowhere else to go other than Palestine. How did this turn of affairs affect the Jewish and Palestinian communities? We will hear the Zionist version first, and then the Palestinian version.

ZIONIST/ISRAELI: The horrifying events in Germany turned out to be a blessing in disguise for the fragile existence of the Zionist movement in Palestine. Most of the refugees, mainly from Germany but also from neighboring countries where anti-Semitic persecution was intensifying, were skilled and educated. German Jews were allowed to bring assets worth a total of 100 million dollars, thanks to the Transfer Agreement reached between the Nazi government and the Zionist movement which was concluded in exchange for lifting a Jewish boycott of Germany.

During the 1930s the Jewish economy in Palestine overtook the Arab sector for the first time, and the Jewish population grew to more than 30 percent of the total population by 1939. In light of the fast economic growth and this rapid population shift over only seven years, combined with considerable expansion of the Zionist movement's military capacities, it became clear to our leaders that the demographic, economic, territorial, and military nucleus necessary for achieving domination over the entire country, or most of it, would soon be in place.

PALESTINIAN: The frustration of the Palestinian population at their leadership's ineffective response over fifteen years of congresses, demonstrations, and futile meetings with stubborn British officials finally led to a massive grassroots uprising. It started with a six-month general strike, one of the longest in colonial history, launched spontaneously by groups of young, urban, middle-class militants all over the country. The strike eventually developed into the great 1936-39 revolt, which was the crucial event of the interwar period in Palestine.

This popular and spontaneous explosion from the bottom up took the British, the Zionists, and the elite Palestinian leadership by surprise. This caused the British to look into the unrest in Palestine. In 1937 a Royal Commission, led by Lord Peel was put in charge. Its proposal was that a small Jewish state, comprising about 17 percent of the territory be established, from which over 200,000 Arabs would be expelled. The rest of the country would remain under British rule or handed over to Britain's client, Amir Abdulla of Transjordan, which to us amounted to much the same thing. Once again, we had been treated as if we had no national existence and no collective rights. The armed revolt that broke out in October 1937 swept the country. It was only brought under control two years later through a massive use of British and Zionist force.

The savage British/Zionist repression, the death and exile of so many Palestinian leaders, and the conflict within our ranks left us divided, without direction, and with our economy debilitated by the time the revolt was crushed in the summer of 1939. This put us in a very weak position to confront the now invigorated Zionist movement, which had gone from strength to strength during the revolt, obtaining lavish amounts of arms and extensive training from the British to help them suppress the uprising.

NARRATOR: As war clouds loomed in Europe in 1939, momentous new global challenges to the British Empire combined with the impact of the Arab revolt, produced a major shift in British policy, away from its previous full-throated support of Zionism. As Europe slid relentlessly toward another world war, the British knew that this conflict would be fought, like the previous one, in part on Arab soil. It was now imperative, in terms of core imperial strategic interests, to improve Britain's image and defuse the fury in the Arab countries and the Islamic world at the forcible repression of the Palestinian revolt, particularly as these areas were being deluged with Axis propaganda about British atrocities in Palestine. A January 1939 report to the cabinet, recommending a change of course in Palestine, stressed the importance of "winning the confidence of Egypt and the neighboring Arab states." To this end, Neville Chamberlain's government issued a White Paper in an attempt to appease outraged Palestinian and Arab opinion. This document called for a severe curtailment of Britain's commitments to the Zionist movement, including strict limits on Jewish immigration.

The Zionists grew more and more hostile to their British patron after the passage of the 1939 White Paper. This hostility erupted with assassinations of British officials and was followed by a sustained campaign of violence against British troops and administrators in Palestine. This culminated in the 1946 blowing up of the British headquarters in Palestine, with the loss of ninety-one lives. Reeling from post-war economic and financial problems, in 1947 the Clement Attlee government dumped the problem of Palestine into the lap of the new United Nations (UN), which formed a UN Special Commission on Palestine (UNSCOP) to provide recommendations for the future of the country.

However, the global landscape had shifted. The dominant powers at the UN were the United States and the Soviet Union, a development the Zionist movement had shrewdly anticipated with its diplomatic efforts toward both, but which left the Palestinians and the Arabs flat-footed. The UNSCOP committee recommended, and the UN voted, to partition Palestine into two separate states—one Jewish, one Arab—in a manner that was exceedingly favorable to the Jewish minority The partition of Palestine into two separate states sounds like the logical solution to the problem, but let's see how the Palestinians viewed the partition plan and then we'll hear the Zionist/Israeli view of the plan.

PALESTINIAN: The partition of Palestine is like the oft-told fable of Solomon. When he was asked to judge which of two women was the real mother of a disputed baby, Solomon suggested cutting the baby in half. The false claimant agreed, but the real mother preferred to lose the baby rather than see it destroyed. A similar scene was reenacted 3,000 years later, except the wisdom of Solomon was lacking. Like the false mother who welcomed the bisection of the child who was not hers, the Zionists accepted partition of the Holy Land because it gave them something they did not own and to which they were not entitled to in justice.

We consistently opposed all partition plans including the one proposed by the Peel Commission in 1937 that would have created a much larger Arab state. The issue was not how much land was awarded to which side. The issue was the injustice of any partition that was dictated by outsiders.

The United Nations was supposedly founded on the principle of national self-determination. All of the great powers gave lip service to this principle. So the alternative to a UN-sponsored partition was obvious. Ask the people of Palestine—Arabs and Jews—what they wanted. The answer would be that they wanted a single state.

But the UN majority thought it would be unsafe and unfair to leave the Jews of Palestine as a minority in an Arab state. The solution they came up with reflected the prevailing anti-Arab racism of the West. As partitioned by the United Nations, the

Jewish state was to have a huge Arab minority, while the proposed Arab state had few Jews. We failed to see why it was not fair for the Jews to be a minority in a unitary Palestinian state, while it was fair for almost half of the Palestinian population—the native majority on its own ancestral soil—to be converted overnight into a minority under alien rule in the envisioned Jewish state. Even if some partition plan might have been acceptable, the UN-proposed division of 1947 was unfair, because it granted 55% of the land to the Jews who constituted 30% of the population.

ZIONIST/ISRAELI: By focusing on the relative Jewish and Arab population figures of 1946-47, the Palestinian argument misunderstands the whole thrust of the story. It was not just the 600,000 Jews then in Palestine who needed a homeland. The Jews of the world needed a homeland if they were to escape eternal oppression and even genocide. The Zionists felt entitled to more than the tiny, fragile state suggested by the UN vote of 1947. Our position was that the Jewish national home promised in both the Balfour Declaration and the League of Nations Mandate for Palestine should cover all of Palestine, which included the land on both sides of the Jordan River.

When Britain separated Jordan from the rest of Palestine, and set it up as an Arab state, they gave away 77% of the Jewish national home. The most militant Zionists refused to accept it. The mainstream Zionist leadership wasn't happy about it either, but accepted it with relatively little complaint and focused their aspirations on the remaining 23%. But it has been our position ever since that Jordan is the Palestinian Arab state. At present, the large majority of its population is Palestinian (estimates range from 60 to 75%). But unfortunately, Israel is the only democracy in the Mideast. The 1947 UN partition would have carved away another 45% of the remainder of Palestine to establish another Palestinian Arab state. Finally, Jerusalem, the historic capital and emotional center of the Jewish nation, was to be excluded from the UN's Jewish state and assigned to international control.

These were wrenchingly difficult concessions for the Zionists. But they did accept them because the overriding need was to establish a Jewish state, to have a place to take in the hundreds of thousands of Jews adrift from the Holocaust, and to have a compromise that would enable the Jewish state to live in peace with its Arab neighbors. The Arabs rejected the partition, not because they didn't like the borders, not because they wanted to have an election first, but because they rejected the existence of a Jewish state. They always have and they still do.

A look at the contemporary reality will show how ridiculous it is to portray Israel, as Arab propaganda does, as a great, powerful expansionist bastion of imperialism that oppresses the Arabs. The 21 Arab states encompass a territory twice the size of the United States with a population of 200 million. The Arabs often claim to be one great nation divided against itself by outside troublemakers. Israel, the only state that belongs to the Jews of the world is the size of New Jersey (even if you include the occupied territories) and has a population approaching five million. Small, surrounded by hostile neighbors, Israel stands ready to accept any Jew and has repeatedly demonstrated its willingness to do so. The rescue of Ethiopian Jews and the unhesitating acceptance of a flood of Russian Jewish refugees are the most recent examples of this. If the Arab states, who claim to love their Palestinian Arab brethren so, would make room for them in a territory more than 600 times the size of Israel, the problem of the Palestinian refugees would be solved. And the Arab world, which possesses 60% of the world's proven oil reserves, can afford it. This doesn't happen because the true, abiding Arab position is that there should be no Jewish state. That is the barrier to peace and that was the basis for Arab rejection of the 1947 partition.

PALESTINIAN: Israel's long-standing suggestion that the Palestinian refugee problem be solved by the dispersion of the Palestinians into the existing Arab states is a continuation of the long-standing Israeli campaign to deny the existence of a Palestinian Arab people. The United Nations has often called on Israel and the Arab states to cooperate to solve the Palestinian refugee problem. They are refugees who obtained that status because of the creation of Israel. And we are not just generic Arabs, who can be consigned to any Arab-speaking region because it suits the convenience of Israel. We are the Arabs who come from Palestine, whose homes and villages and farms and businesses were in Palestine, although most of these have now been systematically destroyed by Israel as part of the effort to wipe them out of history.

The UN majority in 1947 displayed the same lack of regard for the distinct humanity of the Palestinians. The Europeans and Americans who dominated the world in 1947 felt guilty about the Holocaust, because they had let it happen, because it had been done by Western Christians like themselves. But they didn't feel guilty enough to take the Jewish refugees into their own countries. They only felt guilty enough to assign the majority of our homeland to the Jews.

NARRATOR: After all the commotion created by the 1947 UN partition plan, it was never implemented. Instead, despite violent Arab protests, Palestine's Jews proclaimed the creation of the independent state of Israel, comprising more than half of Palestine's territory, on May 15, 1948, the eve of Britain's evacuation. Now all that was left to do was to expel the remaining Arabs. Like a slow, seemingly endless train wreck, the Nakba (Arabic for "catastrophe") unfolded over a period of many months in three phases. In the first phase, before May 15, a pattern of ethnic cleansing resulted in the expulsion and panicked departure of about 3,000 Palestinians along with the devastation of many of their key urban economic, political, civic, and cultural centers. The second phase followed after May 15, when the Israeli army defeated the Arab armies that had joined the war on the side of Palestine. In the wake of the war, and after further massacres of civilians, an even larger number of Palestinians, another 400,000, were expelled and fled from their homes into the neighboring Arab countries and into the West Bank and Gaza (the remaining 22 percent of Palestine that was not conquered by Israel). And none were allowed to return; most of their homes and villages had been destroyed to prevent them from doing so. Israel confiscated the property left by the refugees and redistributed it to Israelis. Palestine no longer existed as a political entity.

Another outcome of the war was that Palestine's so-called allies in the war, Egypt and Jordan, also claimed Palestinian territory; Egypt claimed the Gaza Strip and Jordan, with the help of Britain fought off the Jewish army and claimed what became known as the West Bank and East Jerusalem. Still more Palestinians were expelled from the new state of Israel even after the armistice agreements of 1949 were signed, while further numbers have been forced out since then. In this sense the Nakba can be understood as an ongoing process. The majority of Palestinians now lived in UN-supported refugee camps outside of Palestine, but a substantial minority lived as second-class citizens within the state of Israel. In a third and lasting impact of the Nakba, the victims, the hundred of thousands of Palestinians driven from their homes, served to further destabilize Syria, Lebanon, and Jordan—poor, weak, recently independent countries and the region for years thereafter. First we will hear the Zionist-Israeli reaction to these events and then the Palestinian reaction.

ZIONIST/ISRAELI: Who could have imagined how successful our campaign for control of our sacred land would be? It is not complete, of course, but with God on our side, we know that one day it will be. We will never stop fighting for what God has given us. Like Joshua, our glorious leader from the past, we know that it is imperative that all the infidels and terrorists who hate us and who seek to defile our land must be expelled or exterminated. Only then, can we live in peace and help our oppressed brethren, from any place in the world, find sustenance and peace. We have been truly blessed.

PALESTINIAN: For many reasons, in the bleak new reality after the Nakba, more than a million of us faced a world turned utterly upside down. Wherever we were, whether inside Palestine or not, we experienced profound social disruption. For the majority, this meant destitution—the loss of homes, jobs, and deeply rooted communities. Villagers lost their land and livelihoods and urbanites, their properties and capital, while the Nakba shattered the power of the country's notables together with their economic base. For all of us, no matter our different circumstances, the Nakba formed an enduring touchstone of identity, one that has lasted through several generations. It marked an abrupt collective disruption, a trauma that all of us share in one way or another, personally or through our parents or grandparents. We suddenly had to learn to make our way as a despised minority in a hostile environment as subjects of a Jewish state that has never defined itself as a state of all its citizens.

NARRATOR: Spurred by the unwillingness or inability of the Arab states and the international community to reverse the disastrous consequences of 1948, Palestinian activism did revive in the postbags environment. Small groups engaged in militant activity by taking up arms against Israel. These acts started spontaneously and took several years before such forms of clandestine armed action coalesced into a visible trend and emerged from obscurity with the formation of organizations like Fatah in 1959. The formation of the Palestine Liberation Organization (PLO) by the Arab League in 1964, at the behest of Egypt, was a response to this burgeoning independent Palestinian activism and constituted the most significant attempt by Arab states to control it. Why at the behest of Egypt? Remembering that Egypt had gained control of Gaza in the 1948 Israeli-Arab War, Gaza was now in the forefront of the resistance of Palestinians to their dispossession. Most of the founding leaders of Fatah and the PLO emerged from the cramped quarters of that narrow coastal territory; the militant Popular Front for the Liberation of Palestine (NFLP) drew its most fervent support there; and later on it was the birthplace and stronghold of Islamic Jihad and Hamas, the most strenuous advocates of armed struggle against Israel.

Before moving on to the 1967 war, there is another event that needs to be mentioned: the Suez Crisis. In 1956 Gamel Abdel Nasser of Egypt moved to nationalize the Suez Canal. He also closed the Strait of Tiran which prevented Israeli access to the Gulf of Aqaba. Also it would give Israel a chance to strike back at the militants in Gaza, which it did. Once again, Britain and France allied with Israel—for their own strategic reasons—to invade Egypt and dealt it a crushing blow. The United States, however, had not been advised of their plans and President Eisenhower insisted that the invading nations retreat, which they did. It was not lost on Israel which nation now carried the most clout. From this point on, Israel vigorously pursued a "special relationship" with the United States which inherently included an anti-Palestinian stance. By 1967, there had been a major shift in the United States' relationship with Israel. How did this affect the Zionist movement and the Palestinians? Let's hear from the Zionists first and then from the Palestinians.

ZIONIST/ISRAELI: We had learned our lesson well from our 1956 attempt to invade Egypt. We now knew who was the most powerful nation in the world. We sought and received a green light from Washington to launch a preemptive attack on the air forces of Egypt, Syria, and Jordan. A lightning first strike by our brilliant air force destroyed all of our Arab enemies' airplanes. This gave us complete air superiority, which, in that desert region, in that season, provided an absolute advantage to our ground forces. Our armored columns thus were able to conquer the Sinai Peninsula and the Gaza Strip, the West Bank including Arab East Jerusalem, and the Golan Heights of Syria in six days. All in only six days! Praise be to God and God bless the United States of America!

PALESTINIAN: The resurrection of the idea of Palestine faced an uphill battle in the wake of the 1967 war in most parts of the world. However, there was an important resurgence of Palestinian action. Writers and poets both throughout the Palestinian diaspora and living inside Palestine together with other gifted and engaged artists and intellectuals played a vital role in this renaissance, culturally and politically. Their work helped to reshape a sense of Palestinian identity and purpose that had been tested by the Nakba and the barren years that followed. In novels, short stories, plays, and poetry, they gave us voice to a shared national experience of loss, exile, alienation. At the same time, they evinced a stubborn insistence on the continuity of Palestinian identity and steadfastness in the face of daunting odds.

NARRATOR: The United States reveled in the dramatic Israeli victory in the 1967 six-day war. Besides the amount of territory that changed hands, several things are worth noting. First, the UN in the wake of the war, adopted UN Resolution 242 on November 22, 1967. Like the Balfour Declaration and the Palestinian Mandate before it, it has an anti-Arab/pro-Israel bias. Among other things detrimental to Palestine, it permitted Israel to colonize the now occupied Palestinian territories of the West Bank and Jerusalem and the Gaza Strip.

Second, the PLO which had been under the control of Nasser since its creation in 1964, was taken over by the Palestinians under the leadership of Yassir Arafat. The PLO was based in Lebanon where it oversaw the Palestinian refugee camps in that country. Israel, with the backing of the United States under the Reagan administration, invaded Lebanon in 1982 to achieve its key war aim of dislodging the PLO from Lebanon. The PLO agreed to leave on the condition that the Sabra and Shatila refugee camps would be safe. They were not; Israel orchestrated a bloody massacre soon after the PLO departure. Although the PLO was weakened, this did serve to strengthen the Palestinian movement inside Palestine. Another result of this vicious war was the rise of Hezbollah.

Third, in occupying the West Bank, East Jerusalem, and the Gaza Strip, Israel had also gained for itself a million more Palestinians. These Palestinians, who live under grueling military occupation law, became a source of cheap labor for Israel. They have also become a problem: in 1987 a spontaneous protest against the Israeli occupation broke out in the Gaza strip and spread throughout the occupied territories and Israel proper. It has been called the intifada (Arabic for "uprising"). First we will hear the Zionist/Israeli view of the intifada and then the Palestinian view.

ZIONIST/ISRAELI: In 1987, the intifada was launched, a campaign of terrorism against Israel by the population of the Occupied Territories. We responded with counterterrorism measures, based on a policy of using the least force necessary to pacify the territories. Some expulsions, some detentions, the dynamiting of some houses and some loss of life has occurred. But even in this difficult situation, we have differentiated ourselves from the way such a campaign would be handled in any of the Arab nations.

PALESTINIAN: Equating any Palestinian action to liberate their homeland with "terrorism" is one of the favorite tricks of Israel's leaders. It is doubly ludicrous considering that the two dominant Israeli political leaders of the past 15 years—Prime Ministers Menachem Begin and Yitzhak Shamir—were veteran terrorist leaders in the years leading up to 1948.

When Palestinian children, armed with rocks, seeking to fly their national flag, clash with Israeli soldiers, armed with high-tech weapons, seeking the permanent subjugation and disenfranchisement of two million Arabs, Israel acts hurt and indignant. But, of course, it is Israel that prevents us from expressing our legitimate grievances and aspirations in any peaceful or democratic way. When Israel, with the strongest military in the region, with U.S. arms and subsidies, with a nuclear arsenal, kills far more Arab civilians, women, and children in bombing raids against refugee camps, it is only defending itself.

NARRATOR: PLO leader, Arafat, made the miscalculation of siding with Iraq instead of Kuwait during the first Gulf War (1991) greatly diminishing his status in the Arab world. It happened that this coincided with a moment of American triumphalism, with its victory in Iraq and the end of the Soviet Union. In George H. W. Bush's State of the Union speech in January 1991, he hailed the "new world order" and the "next American century." The Bush administration was determined to take advantage of the opportunity that Saddam's folly (invading Kuwait) had given them to shape and define this new world order. In their view, this necessitated a resolution of the Arab-Israeli conflict. It was in this context that Secretary of State James Baker began planning for a peace conference to be held in Madrid in October 1991, hoping to jump-start direct Israeli-Arab talks and determine the future of Palestine. This did not happen. Attempts again were made in 1993 and 1995 known as the Oslo Accords. America's promise to be an "honest broker" in the talks was simply a lie in deference to their ally, Israel. What were the results of these negotiations? First, let us hear from the Israelis and then the Palestinians.

ZIONIST/ISRAELI: With God's guidance, we do learn from our mistakes. Our leaders realized that the occupied territories —with Israeli troops policing densely populated Palestinian centers simmering with anger—needed modification. Through the peace talks, our leaders designed a way to preserve those parts of the occupation that were advantageous to us—the privileges and prerogatives enjoyed by the state and the settlers—while offloading onerous responsibilities and simultaneously preventing genuine Palestinian self-determination, statehood, and sovereignty. With our creation of the Palestine Authority (PA), the most far-reaching modification was the decision to enlist the PLO as a subcontractor for the occupation. They would be in charge of security which, of course, meant security for us, for the occupation, and for the settlers.

PALESTINIAN: In the quarter-century since the Oslo agreements, the situation in Palestine and Israel has often been falsely described as a clash between two near-equals, between the state of Israel and the quasi-state of the Palestine Authority (PA). This depiction masks the unequal and unchanged colonial reality. The PA has no sovereignty, no jurisdiction, and no authority except that allowed it by Israel. Israel even controls a major part of PA revenues in the form of custom duties and some taxes. Its primary function, to which much of its budget is devoted, is security, but not for our people: it is to provide security for Israel's settlers and occupation forces against the resistance, that is, against their fellow Palestinians. Since 1967, there has been one state authority in all of the territory of Mandatory Palestine: that of Israel. The creation of the PA did nothing to change that reality; it only rearranged the deck chairs on the Palestinian Titanic, while providing Israeli colonization and occupation with an indispensable Palestinian shield. Facing the colossus of the Israeli state is a colonized people denied equal rights and the ability to exercise their right of national self-determination, a continuous condition since the idea of self-determination took hold globally after World War I. But unlike 1947 and 1967, this time our leaders allowed themselves to be drawn into complicity with our adversaries.

NARRATOR: For most Palestinians, deep disappointment with the Oslo Accords set in not long after the 1993 signing ceremony on the White House lawn. The prospect of an end to the military occupation and to the theft of land for Israeli settlements had originally been received with euphoria, and many people believed they were at the beginning of a path leading to statehood. As time went on, there was a dawning realization that despite, and even because of the terms of Oslo, the colonization of Palestine was continuing as before and Israel was no closer to allowing the creation of an independent Palestinian state. In fact, conditions grew much worse for all except for a very small number who were part of the PA who benefitted from normalized relations with Israel. For everyone else, there was consistent denials of permission to travel and move goods from one place to another as an intricate system of permits, checkpoints, walls, and fences was created.

In a conscious Israeli policy of "separation," Gaza was severed from the West Bank, which was itself severed from Jerusalem; jobs within Israel did not return; the settlements and settler-only roads between them proliferated, fragmenting the West Bank in a devastating manner. This post-Oslo confinement was most constricting in the Gaza Strip, which was encircled by troops on land and by the Israeli navy by sea. The conservative Hamas Party, formed in 1987, benefited from the worsening conditions in Palestine and became a serious threat to the Fatah Party and the PLO. Hamas was committed to armed violence and the expulsion of Israel from Palestine.

The worsening situation for Palestinians after Oslo, the fading prospect of statehood, and the intense rivalry between the PLO and Hamas combined to produce the flammable material that erupted into the Second Intifada in September 2000. It was the result of a provocation by Israel and it saw the worst upsurge of violence in the Occupied Territories since 1967. Violence which thereafter spread inside Israel via a wave of deadly suicide bombings. How did the Israelis and Palestinians view these events? First we will hear the Palestinian viewpoint, followed by the Zionist-Israeli viewpoint.

PALESTINIAN: In stark contrast to the First Intifada,, the Second Intifada constituted a major setback for our national movement. The terrible violence of the Second Intafada erased the positive image of us and our cause that had evolved since 1982 and through the First Intafada and the peace negotiations. With horrifying scenes of recurrent suicide bombings transmitting globally (and with this coverage eclipsing that of the much greater violence perpetrated against us), the Israelis ceased to be seen as oppressors, reverting back to the more familiar role of victims of irrational, fanatical terrorists. In addition, in 2002, with their heavy weapons causing widespread destruction, the Israeli army reoccupied the limited areas, mainly cities and towns, that had been evacuated as part of the Oslo Accords, so we even lost the little that we had gained in Oslo.

ZIONIST/ISRAELI: We have had a long-established doctrine of our military, that irrespective of the cost, it must gain the upper hand in any confrontation, and establish its unchallenged capacity not only to deter its enemies, but to crush them. So that is what we did. Their cowardly acts of suicide bombings that killed innocent victims, only served to unify and strength us, while weakening them. The suicide attacks raise serious legal and moral issues, and finally, the world has been able to witness the depravity of our enemy.

NARRATOR: Hamas and Islamic Jihad had boycotted the presidential election of 2005, as they had earlier PA elections, in line with their rejection of the Oslo process (which promised a two-state solution), the Palestinian Authority (PA), and the Palestinian Legislative Assembly (PLA) that had emerged from it. Soon after, however, Hamas performed a surprising U-turn, deciding to run a slate of candidates in the parliamentary elections in January 2006. In its campaign, the organization downplayed the socially conservative Islamic message that had been its trademark, as well as its advocacy of armed resistance to Israel. This act of taking part in the election was a reversal of the greatest significance.

Against all expectations, including its own, Hamas won the elections by a handsome margin. Exit polls after the vote showed that the result owed more to the voters' great desire for change in the Occupied Territories than to a call for Islamic governance or heightened armed resistance to Israel. Many voters simply wanted to throw out the Fatah incumbents, whose strategy of diplomacy had failed and who were seen as corrupt and unresponsive to popular demands.

While Israel vetoed the inclusion of Hamas in a PA coalition, the US subjected Hamas to a boycott. Hamas proceeded to set up its own PA in Gaza. With Hamas now in control of the Gaza Strip, Israel imposed a full-blown siege. Goods entering the strip were reduced to a bare minimum; regular exports were stopped completely; fuel supplies were cut; and leaving and entering Gaza were only rarely permitted. Gaza was in effect turned into an open-air prison. What had begun with international refusal to recognize Hamas's election victory had led to a disastrous Palestinian rupture between the two main political parties as well as the blockade of Gaza. It would provide indispensable international cover for the open warfare that was to come. Israel was able to exploit the deep division among the Palestinians and Gaza's isolation to launch three savage air and ground assaults on the strip that began in 2008 and continued in 2012 and 2014, leaving large swaths of its cities and refugee camps in rubble and struggling with rolling blackouts and contaminated water.

Early on October 7, 2023, Hamas militants led an attack from the Gaza Strip into Israel. More than 1,200 Israelis and foreign nationals were killed. Hamas and other groups also seized 252 hostages. Israel retaliated in a genocidal war against Hamas in Gaza, which is now in its tenth month (July, 2004). Israel and the Palestinians seem to be further away than ever from a lasting and sustainable resolution. There can not be justice for Palestinians nor security for Israelis if this one-hundred plus conflict continues. What a just resolution would take is to dismantle the structures of oppression and supremacy that exist and be based on justice, completely equal rights, and mutual recognition. Israel and the entire Western world must look in the mirror and realize that the violent, discriminatory settler-colonial system—that they have so richly profited from—is the problem. The people of good will and compassion, worldwide, must demand an end to it.

SOURCES:

Parallel Realities by Eric Black

The Hundred Years' War on Palestine by Rashid Khalidi

www.ingramcontent.com/pod-product-compliance
Lightning Source LLC
LaVergne TN
LVHW032006070526
838202LV00058B/6325